At David C Cook, we equip the local church around
the corner and around the globe to make disciples.
Come see how we are working together—go to
www.davidccook.com. Thank you!

DAVID **C** COOK
transforming lives together

HEAVEN

THE OFFICIAL STUDY GUIDE

HEAVEN

THE OFFICIAL STUDY GUIDE

*Offering Peace for Today and
Hope for Tomorrow from the Words of*

RANDY
ALCORN

DAVID C COOK

transforming lives together

HEAVEN
THE OFFICIAL STUDY GUIDE
Published by David C Cook
4050 Lee Vance Drive
Colorado Springs, CO 80918 U.S.A.

Integrity Music Limited, a Division of David C Cook
Brighton, East Sussex BN1 2RE, England

The graphic circle C logo is a registered trademark of David C Cook.

Scripture quotations are taken from the Holy Bible, NEW INTERNATIONAL
VERSION*, NIV*. Copyright © 1973, 2011 by Biblica, Inc. Used by permission.
All rights reserved worldwide. NEW INTERNATIONAL VERSION and NIV
are registered trademarks of Biblica, Inc. * Use of either trademark for the offering
of goods or services requires the prior written consent of Biblica, Inc.

ISBN 978-0-8307-7592-7
eISBN 978-0-8307-7626-9

Material in this resource is adapted from: *Heaven*, by Randy Alcorn.
Copyright © 2004 by Eternal Perspective Ministries. Published by Tyndale
Momentum, Carol Stream, Illinois 60188. Used by permission.

Related titles:
Heaven
Heaven: The Official Study Guide Video Series

All epigraphs and feature quotes within this book, unless otherwise noted,
are excerpted from *Heaven*, by Randy Alcorn.

The Team: Wendi Lord, Nick Lee, Laura Derico, Jack Campbell, Susan Murdock,
JamieLyn Heim, Nick Gilbert, Robb Erickson, Megan Stengel
Cover Design: Nick Lee

Printed in the United States of America
First Edition 2018

3 4 5 6 7 8 9 10 11 12

121319

CONTENTS

HOW THIS WORKS

*Since, then, you have been raised with Christ, set your hearts
on things above, where Christ is seated at the right hand of
God. Set your minds on things above, not on earthly things. For
you died, and your life is now hidden with Christ in God.*

Colossians 3:1–3

When was the last time you thought about Heaven? Often the things that prompt us to think about Heaven are not positive experiences: the death of a loved one, political unrest in the world, troubling criminal acts, and a devastating diagnosis. Perhaps that's why some of us squirm at the idea of studying Heaven. Maybe we're afraid of what we'll discover, or afraid of what we won't.

But followers of Jesus are actually commanded in Scripture to set our hearts and minds on things above—to be heavenly minded. Our lives are not meant to be focused on the troubles of this world as it exists now. Our lives are hidden with Christ—unseen and yet completely real. What better way to be good citizens of Heaven than to study and understand what this kingdom looks like and how we are to live within it?

And what better way to overcome fears about studying Heaven than to begin with the words of the Prince of Peace: "I have told you these things, so that in me you may have peace. In this world you will have trouble. But take heart! I have overcome the world" (John 16:33). Jesus knows about any fear or worry or doubt lingering in our hearts, and He is ready to replace it with assurance and confidence.

We'll be revisiting these promises and many others from God's Word as we engage in this study.

Group Tips

This book is designed to be a simple guide for group discussion and individual reflection as you work through concepts and questions in the more complete resource on the topic, *Heaven*, by Randy Alcorn. Every member of the group would benefit by acquiring a copy of *Heaven* (published by Tyndale), which digs deeper into topics we will discuss, and answers many of the practical questions people have about Heaven. Since our focus is on discovering what God's Word reveals to us about Heaven, the only other book absolutely required for this study is the Bible.

The main goals of this study time are:

- Growth—to get to know members of the body of Christ better and discover ways to serve and stretch one another.
- Understanding—to have a clearer view of what the Bible says about Heaven.
- Peace—to receive assurance about the hope we have for the life to come and how that allows us to walk with peace through a troubled world.
- Perspective—to understand what it means to live with an eternal perspective.

One person may lead the group, or group members may take turns facilitating discussions. No degrees in the study of Heaven are needed. There are instructions throughout this book that will help anyone who is leading to know what to do, with little to no preparation. However, in order to help the group to keep moving, here are some suggestions.

Pray and Read

Before each session, spend some time in prayer and Bible study. Read the Scriptures presented in the session. Test everything that is said—whether in this book, by members of your group, or by your group leader—against Scripture. Be like the Bereans in Acts 17:11, who "received the message with great eagerness and examined the Scriptures every day to see if what Paul said was true."

There are many free online Bible commentaries and dictionaries available that can help as you work through challenging passages. Again, no Bible scholars are required for this study, but it can help you to be confident as a leader (or as a participant in the discussion) if you have a better understanding of what you are reading.

Read over the discussion questions and the chapters of Heaven related to the study. Highlight or take notes on quotes that you find especially helpful or intriguing. Even if every member of the group doesn't have the book, you can share these highlights to enrich the discussion.

In your prayer time, consider the people who will be participating in your group. Even if you don't know them yet, you can pray for them. Pray that any fears or concerns they have about joining in the discussion may be put to rest. Pray that God will increase their compassion for and patience with others, so every member can feel part of the conversation. And pray that their hearts and minds will be open to what God has to say.

Be Mindful

People may come to your group who are grieving the loss of a friend or loved one. Whether you are leading the group or just participating, be mindful of the fact that you could play a helpful role in someone's grieving process (even your own). If someone opens up about their experience, listen respectfully, and resist the urge to offer solutions or overly simplistic answers for the problems and questions they are working through. Many grieving people can experience comfort just in being heard and having a safe space to share.

However, also realize that the purpose of this study has a broader focus. If you are leading the first session, you may want to consult with your pastor to find out about any local grief support programs and counseling services. Share this information with all group members. If discussion veers off course too far into the details of one person's personal experience, you can draw that person back toward the subject at hand by referring to the information that's been provided, and later offering to help the person find professional services or a support group that will be better equipped to offer guidance.

Other people who become increasingly interested in Heaven are those who have just faced or are now facing a potentially fatal health issue. Be respectful of the fact that people who have come close to death or who have received a terminal diagnosis may have a unique and insightful perspective that others can benefit from.

Allow time in your discussion to hear from these voices. Don't be in a hurry to "just get through" to the end of the questions. Leave room for the Holy Spirit to guide your time together. Remember that one of the main goals of this study experience is to understand what it means to live with an eternal perspective—not one that sees value only in what can be accomplished today, but one that understands how God constantly works in and through us to prepare His people for eternity with Him.

Be Practical

Make sure the practical concerns and the physical needs of your group members are met. Agree on a time and place to meet and then communicate that information carefully to all members. Make sure your meeting place can accommodate any members of your group who have limited mobility or other challenging physical circumstances. Talk with your group about how you can offer childcare—you may wish to share in the cost of hiring a babysitter for your time together, or you may want to take turns supervising children in a separate room from the study group. Think about the ways your group can be welcoming to anyone who wishes to attend.

Bring extra paper and pens and flat surfaces (books, trays, etc.) to write on, if needed. Bring Bibles to share. You might want to supply a variety of Bibles translations so people can compare them.

Group members will benefit from each having their own copy of *Heaven: The Official Study Guide*. If possible, you might want to have a few extra guides available in case other people decide to join the study later, or in case members bring guests.

The accompanying video to this study is *Heaven: The Official Study Guide Video Series*. In this resource you will find teaching for each of the six sessions, facilitator notes, and a worship song lyric video for each session. This video is available for purchase as a DVD or as downloadable files. Make sure you have the appropriate equipment for playback (either a device able to play DVDs or a computer to play the downloadable files) for each meeting.

Session Structure

Each session includes time to connect with God, with His Word, and with each other. Here's how a typical session is structured.

PREPARATION
Look here to find out what you can do to be ready for the next session: Scriptures to read, corresponding chapters from *Heaven*, prayer, group-related notes, etc.

CONNECTION (5–10 Minutes)
Open with prayer and a question or two to get everyone talking.

VIDEO TEACHING (10–15 Minutes)

If you have the *Heaven: The Official Study Guide Video Series*, watch the corresponding teaching session. You may wish to use the provided worship song at the beginning of your time to focus attention or at the end to offer space for reflection—or both!

DISCUSSION (30 Minutes)

Each session includes questions to guide your group members to read Scripture, share thoughts, and gain a better understanding of the concepts being presented.

REFLECTION (5–10 Minutes)

Use this time for prayer, for praise (using the worship song), or to meditate on God's Word (Scripture references provided).

RESPONSE

During the time that follows your group meeting, read through the Scriptures that were presented and write about your own conclusions or questions. Prompts and questions have been provided to get you started, and there is space for you to record your thoughts. Even if you are not typically a "journaler," go ahead and jot down

SESSION STRUCTURE

Preparation
Connection
Video Teaching
Discussion
Reflection
Response

some notes—it will help you remember what you're learning. And if you share your thoughts in the next group session, it could help other members understand something better.

Eternal Thinking

In the introduction to Randy Alcorn's book *Heaven*, he talks about the terminal disease of mortality. Our death rate is 100 percent—everyone's life as it exists now on Earth will at some point come to an end. Whether we die or Jesus comes first, the life we have known will stop and something different will happen. We can try to ignore it, but the fact of death does not go away. And it's better not to ignore it, but to face it, talk about it, and think about it.

No one is ever really prepared for that moment when we lose a loved one—and preparation doesn't ever let us skip the grieving process. In fact, we can learn a lot through our grief, as we'll talk about in this study. But we can prepare for the life to come. Our choices here matter. How we grow now as followers of Jesus matters. As we study Scripture and consider eternity carefully, we'll find there are truths that we can hold on to that will help us to find peace, hope, and even joy in some of life's most difficult times.

If you are a reader of Randy's blog (www.epm.org/blog), you probably know that Randy's wife and best friend, Nanci, was diagnosed with cancer early in 2018. During that time Randy wrote:

Nanci and I talk often of God's grace and sovereignty and are thankful we can fully trust Him with whatever is ahead of us. Several months ago, she wrote this prayer based on Psalm 23. It spoke to me, and I hope it speaks to you too, as you reflect on your heavenly Shepherd and the ways He leads and cares for you through every circumstance in your life here on Earth, and the promise He offers for the life to come. Read Psalm 23 first (presented on the following page), then enter into Nanci's prayer.

Psalm 23

The LORD is my shepherd, I lack nothing.
    He makes me lie down in green pastures,
he leads me beside quiet waters,
    he refreshes my soul.
He guides me along the right paths
    for his name's sake.
Even though I walk
    through the darkest valley,
I will fear no evil,
    for you are with me;
your rod and your staff,
    they comfort me.
You prepare a table before me
    in the presence of my enemies.
You anoint my head with oil;
    my cup overflows.
Surely your goodness and love will follow me
    all the days of my life.
and I will dwell in the house of the LORD forever.

Nanci's Prayer

Please, Shepherd of my life,

- Cause me to want nothing more—not even good health—than to have You as my Shepherd.
- Reveal to me that the pastures and waters to which You lead me are green and still—because You are there!
- Engage my heart to receive the restoration of my soul by Your Holy Spirit.
- Renew my conviction that, for Your name's sake, righteousness is the direction of each path You have for me.
- May Your Holy Spirit—the Comforter—banish all my fears of evil (being out of control, letting pride inflate me, weakness, pain, loss of plans) as I walk through this valley—because You are with me!
- Open my eyes and my ears to the protection and comfort of Your rod and staff. Don't let me miss those things and people which You have provided me for this purpose.
- Help me experience the table You have prepared for me in the presence of this cancer.
- Don't let me overlook—or fail to ask for—Your every healing drop of oil on my head.
- Keep my perspective on my daily overflowing cup of Your goodness and mercy.
- Direct my longing toward my place in Your house, forever!

WHAT IS HEAVEN?

Let us hold unswervingly to the hope we profess, for he who promised is faithful.
Hebrews 10:23

Preparation

Concepts in this session are covered in the Introduction and Chapters 1 and 2 of *Heaven*. We'll also be studying the following Scriptures: Exodus 15:12–13; Mark 16:19–20; Luke 2:14; John 14:1–4; 1 Thessalonians 4:15–17; Hebrews 4:14, 9:24, 11:13–16; Revelation 3:11–13; Philippians 1:19–23 and 2 Corinthians 5:1–9; John 8:44 and Revelation 13:1–6; 1 Corinthians 2:9–13 and Deuteronomy 29:29; Colossians 3:1–3.

Leader tip: Communicate with your group to make sure they are aware of the above resources. If you will be using the video teaching and/or the worship song provided on the *Heaven: The Official Study Guide Video Series*, check to see if the host of the group has appropriate video equipment.

Connection

As you begin this session, let a volunteer open with a brief prayer for your time together. If group members don't know each other well, invite members to share their names and the best vacation locations they've ever visited. If you have a large group, you may want to divide into smaller groups of two or three for the Connection activity.

Ask the groups to talk about their answers to these questions, then let some share the highlights of those discussions with the entire gathering:

- Imagine you are five years old again. What was your concept of Heaven at that time?
- Where did your perception of Heaven come from?
- How has your concept of Heaven changed from when you were a child? What accounts for these changes?

Video Teaching

If you have the *Heaven: The Official Study Guide Video Series*, watch Session 1 now. Before pressing play, make sure everyone is in a position from which they can see and hear the video well. You may wish to use the provided worship song at the beginning of your time to focus attention or at the end to offer space for reflection—or both!

Discussion

The sense that we will live forever somewhere has shaped every civilization in human history. Anthropological evidence suggests that every culture has a God-given, innate sense of the eternal—that this world is not all there is.

Yet a startling thing has happened among modern Western Christians. Many of us habitually think and act as if there were no eternity—or as if what we do in this present life has no eternal consequences. The trend is to focus on our present circumstances instead of our eternal future. Because the topic of Heaven is so rarely addressed, and because of pervasive distortions of what it is like, it's common for Christians to not look forward to Heaven—or even to dread it. How sad!

The goal of this session is to center our thoughts on what Scripture has to say about our eternal home.

1. From the Bible, the video teaching, or the *Heaven* book, offer two statements of what Heaven is:

   a)

   b)

2. Read Exodus 15:12–13; Mark 16:19–20; Luke 2:14; John 14:1–4; 1 Thessalonians 4:15–17; Hebrews 4:14, 9:24, 11:13–16; Revelation 3:11–13. Write down what these verses say to you about characteristics of Heaven.

3. Think and talk about these questions: In what ways is Heaven described as a place? Is it described as being different from other places? How?

We were made for a person and a place. Jesus is that person and Heaven is that place. When Jesus told His disciples, "In my Father's house are many rooms. . . . I am going there to prepare a place for you" (John 14:2), He deliberately chose common, physical terms (*house, rooms, place*) to describe where He was going and what He was preparing for us. He wanted to give His disciples (and us) something tangible to look forward to—an actual place where they (and we) would go to be with Him.

Physically resurrected people need a physical place to live, not an ethereal realm of disembodied spirits. Human beings are not suited for such a realm. A *place* is by nature physical, just as human beings are by nature physical. (We are also spiritual.) What we are suited for—what we've been specifically designed for—is a place like the one God made for us: Earth.

In this study, we'll see from Scripture an exciting yet strangely neglected truth—that God never gave up on His original plan for human beings to dwell on Earth. In fact, the climax of history will be the creation of new heavens and a New Earth (Revelation 21:1-4).

4. When people express worries about going to Heaven and living there eternally, what are they sometimes concerned about? What assumptions do they make about Heaven?

5. Read the words of the following quote from the church father
    Cyprian and then look up Philippians 1:19–23 and 2 Corinthians
    5:1–9.

    Let us greet the day which assigns each of us to his own
    home, which snatches us from this place and sets us free
    from the snares of the world, and restores us to paradise and
    the kingdom. Anyone who has been in foreign lands longs
    to return to his own native land. . . . We regard paradise as
    our native land.

    From the words of Cyprian and the words of Paul, what do the
    longings we have now reveal to us about what we might experience
    in Heaven?

6. Consider the idea that Paul speaks of dying and being with Christ as "better by far." What does it mean to you to think of living in Heaven as being better by far than your current experience? List out some of your present circumstances. Beside each item on your list, describe something that would be "better by far" than your current situation.

Better by far

Trying to develop an appetite for a disembodied existence in a non-physical Heaven is like trying to develop an appetite for gravel. No matter how sincere we are, and no matter how hard we try, it's not going to work. Nor should it.

What God made us to desire, and therefore what we do desire if we admit it, is exactly what He promises to those who follow Jesus Christ: a resurrected life in a resurrected body, with the resurrected Christ on a resurrected Earth. Our desires correspond precisely to God's plans. It's not that we want something, so we engage in wishful thinking that what we want exists. It's the opposite—the reason we want it is precisely because God has planned for it to exist.

Nineteenth-century British theologian J. C. Ryle said, "I pity the man who never thinks about heaven" (*Heaven*, Christian Focus Publications, 2000, p. 19). We could also say, "I pity the man who never thinks accurately about Heaven." It's our inaccurate thinking, I believe, that causes us to choose to think so little about Heaven.

Let's consider the forces at work behind our misconceptions and inaccurate thinking about Heaven, and learn how to counteract those.

7. Read John 8:44, Revelation 13:1–6. How does Jesus characterize the devil? What are the three objects of slander for the satanic beast described in Revelation 13?

8. It's clear from Scripture that Satan lies. Some of his favorite lies are about Heaven. Consider this: If we become convinced that Heaven is boring, unearthly, or unknowable, what impact does that have on our motivation to live for the next life? How can it affect how (or whether) we share our faith?

Another source of our misconceptions about Heaven is naturalism—the belief that the world can be understood in scientific terms, without recourse to spiritual or supernatural explanations. We succumb to naturalistic assumptions that what we see is real and what we don't see isn't. Therefore, Heaven can't be real because we can't see it.

The blind must take by faith that there are stars in the sky. If they depend on their ability to see, they will conclude there are no stars. We will one day be delivered from the blindness that separates us from the real world. We'll realize then the stupefying bewitchment we've lived under. By God's grace, may we clearly see the liberating truth about Christ the King and Heaven, His Kingdom.

9. Read 1 Corinthians 2:9–13 and Deuteronomy 29:29. How might people sometimes use 1 Corinthians 2:9 and Deuteronomy 29:29a as arguments that we can't know anything about what Heaven is like? How does the context of these verses provide a counterargument to that idea?

10. Read the command in Colossians 3:1–3. The Greek word translated "set your hearts on" is *zeteo*, which is in the present tense, suggesting an ongoing process and could be translated as, "Keep seeking Heaven." It is a diligent, active, single-minded investigation. So

we can understand Paul's admonition in Colossians 3:1 as follows: "Diligently, actively, single-mindedly pursue the things above"— in a word, *Heaven*. Given how this term is used, how do you think Paul is suggesting we should think about Heaven? What have you been doing daily to set your mind on things above? What should you do differently?

11. The command to set our hearts and minds on Heaven implies that this is not something we naturally or easily do—we have to be reminded and directed to do it. Our minds are often caught up in earthly things. Consider the metaphor of the dot and the line, as presented in the video teaching. Our present life on earth is the dot. It begins. It ends. It's brief. However, from the dot, a line extends that goes on forever. That line is eternity, which Christians will spend in Heaven. Right now we're living in the dot. But what are we living for? The shortsighted person lives for the dot. The person with perspective lives for the line. Fill the "dot" on the following page up with things that take your mind away from heavenly things. What makes the things in the dot so effective at taking our focus away from eternity? In what ways can we set our hearts on Heaven and live for the line?

Reflection

You may wish to use a worship song ("Great I Am" is provided on the video resource) to help the group focus as they spend a few minutes reflecting on Heaven. Here are some Scriptures and thoughts to help you:

- Think again about that image you had of Heaven when you were a small child. Picture it in your mind. Now, considering what we've learned so far about Heaven together, what would you change? Adjust your image to better reflect the biblical presentation of Heaven.
- Read Colossians 3:1–3 again. What can you do this week to become more heavenly minded?

- Pray, asking God to help you weed out any misconceptions and to reveal your fears and doubts about Heaven.
- Commit to reading the Scriptures presented below.

Response

Use the ideas and questions presented here in your personal time with God this week:

- What is one thought from this session that has given you some peace or made something clearer to you about Heaven?

- Read the descriptions of Heaven as presented in the following verses and jot down any thoughts you have as you reflect on these verses:

  Isaiah 25:8–12

  John 14:2–4

  Hebrews 12:22–23

Revelation 7:13–17

Revelation 22:3–7

- Use Ephesians 1:17–23 to guide your prayer time. Ask your Father God for the Spirit of wisdom and revelation, so you can know Him more. Ask for your heart to be opened up to the hope you have in the riches of His glorious inheritance and in His incomparably great power. Thank God for raising Christ from the dead and submit your will to His authority. And ask God to help you serve through the body of Christ.

NEW HEAVEN AND NEW EARTH

*But in keeping with his promise we are looking forward to a
new heaven and a new earth, where righteousness dwells.*

2 Peter 3:13

Preparation

Concepts in this session are covered in depth in Chapters 8–12 of *Heaven*.
Details about the present Heaven and distinctions between it and the future
Heaven can be found in Chapters 5–7, some of which will be addressed in later
sessions as well. If you have time before the session, review the "Three Eras of
Mankind and Earth" chart that appears at the end of this session (it also appears
in Chapter 8 of *Heaven*). We'll also be studying the following Scriptures:
Ecclesiastes 12:7; Luke 16:22–31, 23:43; Philippians 1:20–23; 2 Corinthians
5:1–10; Revelation 6:9–11; 1 Thessalonians 4:13–18; Romans 8:1–27; Acts
3:21; Isaiah 11:6–10, 25:6–8, 62, 65:17–25; Revelation 21 and 22.

Leader tip: Communicate with your group to make sure they are aware
of these resources. If you will be using the video teaching and/or the worship
song provided on the *Heaven: The Official Study Guide Video Series*, check to
see if the host of the group has appropriate video equipment.

Connection

As you begin this session, let a volunteer open with a brief prayer for your time together. If there are newcomers, introduce them to the group. If you have a large group, you may want to divide into smaller groups of two or three people for the Connection activity.

Ask the groups to talk about their answers to these questions, then let some share the highlights of those discussions with the entire gathering:

- Have you ever been in a place that felt like "paradise" to you? What about the place created that effect?

Video Teaching

If you have the *Heaven: The Official Study Guide Video Series*, watch Session 2 now. Before pressing play, make sure everyone is in a position from which they can see and hear the video well. You may wish to use the provided worship song at the beginning of your time to focus attention or at the end to offer space for reflection—or both!

Discussion

In Session 1, we talked about some misconceptions we have about Heaven and how Scripture can help us overcome them. Before we dive into a deeper discussion of the present Heaven and the future Heaven, which is called the New Earth, it's important to make sure everyone understands that Heaven is *not* our default destination. Many books on Heaven seem to assume every reader is Heaven-bound. The Bible says otherwise.

What would keep us out of Heaven is universal: "All have sinned and fall short of the glory of God" (Romans 3:23). Sin separates us from a relationship with God (Isaiah 59:2). God is so holy that He cannot allow sin into His presence: "Your eyes are too pure to look on evil; you cannot tolerate wrong" (Habakkuk 1:13). Because we are sinners, we are not entitled to enter God's presence. We cannot enter Heaven as we are.

No one goes to Heaven automatically. Unless our sin problem is resolved, the only place we will go is our true default destination . . . Hell.

Earth is an in-between world touched by both Heaven and Hell. Earth leads directly into Heaven or directly into Hell, affording a choice between the two. For Christians, this present life is the closest they will come to Hell. For unbelievers, it is the closest they will come to Heaven.

The reality of the choice that lies before us in this life is both wonderful and awful. Given the reality of our two possible destinations, shouldn't we be willing to pay any price to avoid Hell and go to Heaven? And yet, the price has already been paid. "You were bought at a price" (1 Corinthians 6:20). The price paid was exorbitant—the shed blood of God's Son, Jesus Christ.

Consider the wonder of it: God determined that He would rather go to Hell on our behalf than live in Heaven without us.

A pardon must be accepted. Similarly, Christ offers each of us the gift of forgiveness and eternal life—but just because the offer is made doesn't make it ours. To have it, we must choose to accept it.

1. Have you confessed your sins? asked Christ to forgive you? placed your trust in Christ's death and resurrection on your behalf? asked Jesus to be your Lord and empower you to follow Him? Wouldn't it be tragic if you read this book on Heaven but didn't get to go there? Use the space below to write about what you believe about Jesus Christ.

2. One of the big questions many people have is, "What happens when we die?" What are some common answers people have?

3. Read Ecclesiastes 12:7; Luke 16:22–31, 23:43; Philippians 1:20–23; 2 Corinthians 5:1–10; and Revelation 6:9–11. What answers does the Bible offer to this question of what happens when we die?

Theologians refer to the period between the believer's life on Earth, and our resurrection to life on the New Earth, as the intermediate Heaven. I prefer the term *present Heaven*, as most people find it less confusing. It's the period and place in which we live, between physical death and resurrection.

Read 1 Thessalonians 4:13–18. Because of the reference to falling asleep, some believe that the time in the present Heaven will be a time of unconsciousness.

But sleep here is a euphemism for death, a temporary condition to be followed by rising up to resume life. We know this because of other passages. Christ depicted Lazarus in Heaven and the rich man in Hell as conscious immediately after they died (Luke 16:22-31). Jesus told the dying thief on the cross, "Today you will be with me in paradise" (Luke 23:43). The apostle Paul says that to die is to be with Christ (Philippians 1:23) and to be absent from the body is to be present with the Lord (2 Corinthians 5:8).

These passages make clear that there is no "soul sleep" at our deaths, but there's a relocation either to the present Heaven or Hell.

Usually when we refer to "Heaven," we mean the place that Christians go when they die. This is the *present* or intermediate Heaven. When we tell our children "Grandma's now in Heaven," that's what we're talking about.

By definition, an intermediate state or location is *temporary*. Life in the Heaven we go to when we die, where we'll dwell prior to our bodily resurrection, is "better by far" than living here on Earth under the curse, away from the direct presence of God (Philippians 1:23). Still, the intermediate or present Heaven is *not* our final destination.

Some, such as theologian N. T. Wright, argue that the New Earth shouldn't be called Heaven. But it seems clear to me that God's special dwelling place is by definition Heaven, and we're told that "the dwelling of God" will be with mankind on the redeemed Earth (Revelation 21:3). So the present Heaven and the New Earth will be essentially the same place.

We must not lose sight of our true destination. If we do, we'll be confused and disoriented in our thinking about where, and in what form, we will spend eternity.

4. Look at the "Three Eras of Mankind and Earth" chart (shown in part in the video teaching and appearing at the end of this session chapter). What connections between the past, present, and future stand out to you?

5. Read Romans 8:1–17 as a group. Work together (in pairs or small groups) to come up with two lists. One list will record the various ways that living according to the flesh is described. The other list should describe the qualities and results of living by the Spirit. How does life in the Spirit compare to what you think life might be like in Heaven?

6. Read Romans 8:18–27 together. How is "the creation" described in
    these verses? What is the creation waiting for? What hints do you
    see that Jesus didn't come into the world to redeem only humans,
    but to redeem the whole world? Why is this point important?

7. Read Romans 8:28. How does knowing that God is sovereign over
    the world and everything in it, and has plans to redeem that whole
    world, affect your understanding of this often-quoted Bible verse?

The entire physical universe was created for God's glory. But humanity rebelled, and the universe fell under the weight of our sin. Yet the serpent's seduction of Adam and Eve did not catch God by surprise. He had in place a plan by which He would redeem mankind—and all of creation—from sin, corruption, and death. Just as He promises to make men and women new, He promises to renew the earth itself.

> See, I will create new heavens and a new earth. (Isaiah 65:17)

> "As the new heavens and the new earth that I make will endure before me," declares the Lord, "so will your name and descendants endure." (Isaiah 66:22)

> In keeping with his promise we are looking forward to a new heaven and a new earth, where righteousness dwells. (2 Peter 3:13)

> Then I saw "a new heaven and a new earth," for the first heaven and the first earth had passed away. (Revelation 21:1)

Christ's mission is both to redeem what was lost in the Fall and to destroy all competitors to God's dominion, authority, and power. When everything is put under His feet, when God rules all and mankind rules the earth as kings under Christ, the King of kings, at last all will be as God intends. The period of rebellion will be over forever, and the universe, and all who serve Christ, will participate in the Master's joy!

Let's look at verses that can help us understand more about the future Heaven—the New Earth.

8. We long for a return to Paradise—to a perfect world, where God walks with us and talks with us. And that is exactly what God promises. Read Acts 3:21 and Isaiah 11:6–10, 25:6–8, 62, 65:17–25. What does the prophet Isaiah tell us about God's plans to restore "everything"? From these verses, what is included in that "everything"?

9. Read Revelation 21 and 22. Look for the details that tell us how this New Earth will resemble what we are familiar with now. What will be different? In what ways is Eden going to be restored?

10. Review the "Three Eras of Mankind and Earth" chart. Consider the parallels between the past, present, and future existence of mankind and our relationship with God as our creator, our sustainer, and our redeemer. What does it mean to you that the themes present in this chart exist and run through the entire story of mankind? What does it tell you about God?

Reflection

You may wish to use a worship song ("Offering" is provided on the video resource) to allow the group to spend a few minutes reflecting on Heaven. Here are some Scriptures and thoughts to help you focus:

- What does the idea of a redeemed and renewed Earth mean for you? Does it change anything about how you feel about the end of your life on Earth now?
- Read Isaiah 60:18–22. What feelings or thoughts do these verses stir in you?
- Pray, asking God to continue to reveal the truth of His Word to you. Thank God for His promises to renew and redeem and restore us and the Earth.
- Commit to reading the Scriptures presented below.

Response

Use the ideas and questions presented here in your personal time with God this week:

- What is one thought from this session that has given you some peace or made something clearer to you about Heaven?

- Read Genesis 1 and 2 then compare what you find with Revelation 21 and 22. What connections do you see? What does that say to you about God's plan?

- Read 2 Corinthians 5:16–21 and use it to guide your prayer time. Thank God for His plan to renew all things and for His transforming you into a new creation. Ask Him to help you change how you look at others and to see them as the new creations they can be in Christ. Ask Him for opportunities to speak and act as His ambassador.

Three Eras of Mankind and Earth

PAST Genesis 1–2	PRESENT Genesis 3–Revelation 20	FUTURE Revelation 21–22
Original mankind	Fallen mankind; some believe and are transformed	Resurrected mankind
Original Earth	Fallen Earth, with glimmers of original	New (resurrected) Earth
God delegates reign to innocent mankind	Disputed reign with God, Satan, and fallen mankind	God delegates reign to righteous mankind
Mankind given dominion, with intended stewardship of Earth	Mankind's dominion thwarted, frustrated, and twisted	Mankind's dominion fulfilled; redeemed stewardship of Earth
God in Heaven, visiting Earth	God in Heaven, separate yet active (indwells believers by His Spirit)	God living forever with mankind on the New Earth
No Curse (universal perfection and blessing)	Sin and the Curse (withdrawal of blessing, or blessing selectively given, plus common grace)	No more Curse (greater blessing, deeper perfection, grace unending)
No shame	Shame	No shame or potential for shame
Tree of life in Eden (mankind can eat)	Tree of life in Paradise (mankind cut off from)	Tree of life in New Jerusalem (mankind can eat again forever)
River of life	Rivers and nature, with glimmers of past and future	River of life flows from the throne
Before redemption	Unfolding drama of redemption	After redemption
Sin unknown	Sin corrupts; its power and penalty assaulted, defeated by Christ	Sin forever removed

PAST **Genesis 1–2**	**PRESENT** **Genesis 3–Revelation 20**	**FUTURE** **Revelation 21–22**
No death	Death permeates all	Death forever removed
Mankind created from the earth	Mankind dies, returns to the earth; new life to some	Mankind resurrected from the earth to live on the New Earth
First Adam reigns	First Adam falls; mankind reigns corruptly, with glimpses of good; second Adam comes	Last Adam reigns as God-man, with mankind as co-heirs and delegated kings
Serpent/Satan on Earth	Serpent/Satan judged but still present	Serpent/Satan removed from Earth, thrown into eternal fire
God walking with humans in the Garden	Humans cut off from God	God dwells face-to-face with humans
God's glory evident to all, in all	God's glory obscured, seen in glimpses	God's glory forever manifested in all
Unhindered individual worship	Worship hampered by sin	Unhindered corporate worship
God's goodness known	God's goodness known by some, doubted by others	God's goodness forever celebrated
Creation and mankind perfect	Creation and mankind tainted by sin	Creation and mankind restored to perfection
Mankind names, tends, rules the animals	Animals and mankind hurt each other	Animals and mankind live in complete harmony
Ground fertile, vegetation lush	Ground cursed, vegetation diseased	Ground fertile, vegetation thrives
Abundant food and water	Hunger and thirst, toil for food and water	Abundant food and water

PAST Genesis 1–2	PRESENT Genesis 3–Revelation 20	FUTURE Revelation 21–22
Restfulness, satisfaction in labor	Restlessness, toil in labor	Enhanced restfulness, joy in labor
Innocence, closeness to God	Sin (alienation from God); some declared righteous in Christ	Righteousness (intimacy with God); complete righteousness in Christ
Paradise	Paradise lost, sought; glimmers seen, foretastes	Paradise regained and magnified
Mankind in ideal place	Mankind banished, struggles and wanders in fallen place(s)	Mankind restored to ideal place
Mankind able either to sin or not to sin	Mankind enslaved to sin, empowered not to sin	Mankind unable to sin, permanently empowered
Naked in innocence	Clothed due to unrighteousness	Clothed with righteousness
One marriage (Adam and Eve)	Many marriages	One marriage (Christ and church)
Marriage perfect	Marriage flawed by sin, blame, manipulation	Marriage perfect, unhindered
Beginning of human culture	Contamination and advancement of culture	Purification and eternal expansion of culture
Mankind learns, creates in purity	Mankind learns, creates in impurity (Cain, Babel)	Mankind learns, creates in wisdom and purity
Mankind rules and expands Paradise	Mankind banished from Paradise, longs for return to Paradise	Mankind has unlimited, free access to Paradise
God's plan for mankind and Earth revealed	God's plan delayed and enriched	God's plan for mankind and Earth realized

LIVING WITH GOD

Look! God's dwelling place is now among the people, and he will dwell with them. They will be his people, and God himself will be with them and be their God.

Revelation 21:3

Preparation

Concepts in this session are covered in depth in Chapters 17–19 of *Heaven*. We'll also be studying the following Scriptures: Psalm 63:1; Revelation 22:4; Exodus 33:18–23; John 1:18; 1 Timothy 6:15–16; Hebrews 12:14; Job 19:1–27; Romans 1:20; Psalm 19:1; 1 Timothy 4:1–8; Jeremiah 31:31–34; Leviticus 26:9–13; Ezekiel 37:24–28; 2 Corinthians 6:14–18; Revelation 21:1–4, 22–27; 22:12–14; Isaiah 25:6–8; Matthew 20:25–28; Luke 12:37; John 13:3–17; Genesis 47:31; Exodus 33:9–11; 1 Kings 1:46–48; Nehemiah 9:3; Daniel 7:13–14; 1 Thessalonians 5:16–18; and Revelation 4–5, 7:9–12.

Leader tip: Communicate with your group to make sure they are aware of these resources. If you will be using the video teaching and/or the worship song provided on the *Heaven: The Official Study Guide Video Series*, check to see if the host of the group has appropriate video equipment.

Connection

As you begin this session, have a volunteer open with a brief prayer for your time together. If there are newcomers, introduce them to the group. If you have a large group, you may want to divide into smaller groups of two or three for the Connection activity.

Ask the groups to talk about their answers to these questions, then let some share the highlights of those discussions with the entire gathering:

- Have you ever been reunited with someone you care about—someone you haven't seen in a long time? What did that feel like? What was good about it? What was disappointing?

Video Teaching

If you have the *Heaven: The Official Study Guide Video Series*, watch Session 3 now. Before pressing play, make sure everyone is in a position from which they can see and hear the video well. You may wish to use the provided worship song at the beginning of your time to focus attention or at the end to offer space for reflection—or both!

Discussion

By now you will have noticed some recurring themes—that Heaven is a real place, with both physical and spiritual aspects, that Heaven is the dwelling place of God, and that God's eternal plan for us includes a full restoration, rather than the abandonment, of Earth. Now, had I been dealing with aspects of Heaven in order of their importance, I would have begun with a chapter about God and our relationship with Him and what the Bible tells us about that in the context of eternity. However, I thought it was first necessary to establish a picture of our physical, resurrected life on the New Earth. If we don't base our perspective of Heaven on a clear understanding of our coming bodily resurrection and the truth about the physical nature of the New Earth, our concept of being with God will be more like that of Eastern mysticism than of biblical Christianity.

The presence of God is the essence of Heaven. As John Milton put it, "Thy presence makes our Paradise, and where Thou art is Heaven." Heaven will be a physical extension of God's goodness.

Psalm 63:1 says, "You, God, are my God, earnestly I seek you; I thirst for you, my whole being longs for you, in a dry and parched land where there is no water." We may imagine we want a thousand different things, but God is the one we really long for. His presence brings satisfaction; His absence brings thirst and longing. *Our longing for Heaven is a longing for God*—a longing that involves not only our inner beings, but our bodies as well. Being with God is the heart and soul of Heaven. Every other heavenly pleasure will derive from and be secondary to His presence. God's greatest gift to us is, and always will be, Himself.

1. Revelation 22:4 tells us that, on the New Earth, God's servants will see His face. We may have heard this phrase before, but let's consider for a moment how amazing—even shocking—this idea is. Read Exodus 33:18–23; John 1:18; 1 Timothy 6:15–16; and Hebrews 12:14. What can we see from these verses about the experience of seeing God?

2. Read Job 19:25–27. Consider how Job is yearning to see God and calls Him "redeemer." Now go back and read verses 1–24. Remember, Job was experiencing extreme suffering and loss. What does it say to you that Job yearns to see God at this time?

We need not wait until the New Earth to catch glimpses of God. We're told His "invisible qualities" can be "clearly seen" in "what has been made" (Romans 1:20). Yes, we live amid devastation, and we know the corruption of our own hearts. Yes, our vision is hampered by the curse that affects all of creation. Eden has been trampled, torched, and savaged. Nevertheless, the stars in the sky declare God's glory (Psalm 19:1); in our own bodies we can see the intricacy of God's craftsmanship; and in flowers and rain and art and music we see vestiges of God's beauty and creativity. And one day the curse of sin will be reversed. One day, both we and the universe will be forever set free. In that day, *we will see God.*

As Augustine prayed in *The Confessions*, "You have made us for yourself, and our hearts are restless until they rest in you."

3. Sometimes now, people worry about letting the things we desire— even the good things—become greater to us than our desire for God. And on an earth that is filled with sin, this is a valid concern. But read 1 Timothy 4:1–8. What do these verses tell us about the good things God created? What kind of training holds promise for the life to come?

4. Scripture shows us that God intends for us to enjoy the good gifts He has given us. If we know this is true for our lives now, what does this tell us about our lives with Him in Heaven?

5. Read Jeremiah 31:31–34. Bring to mind the most fascinating person you know. Or think about what it was like when you first fell in love with someone. Would you ever get bored of talking with that person? Would you ever feel like you had known all there was to know of his or her thoughts, feelings, and perspectives? Write about your experience of being with someone you love, or write about your imagined experience with someone you would like to meet.

6. If you had the opportunity to spend the evening with any person who's ever lived, whom would you choose?

7. Now imagine what it must be like to know the infinite person of God and be able to talk with Him. Who is more beautiful, talented, knowledgeable, fascinating, and interesting than He? How does this change or shape your idea of what it might be like to be with Him in Heaven?

The good news is, God chose you. If you're a Christian, you'll be with Him for eternity and enjoy endless fascinating conversations and experiences. Incredibly, He'll also enjoy your company and mine. After all, He paid the ultimate price—just so He could have us over to His place for eternity.

We can learn about the relationship we will have with God on the New Earth by looking at how Jesus interacted with His first disciples. When we look in the Gospels, we see that the disciples laughed and cried and ate and drank with Jesus. They walked dusty roads and rode in boats with Him. They asked Him questions and learned from Him.

Jesus told His disciples, "Let me teach you" (Matthew 11:29). In Heaven we'll have the privilege of listening to Jesus teach while we sit at His feet as Mary did (Luke 10:39). We'll also enjoy walking with Him over the country-side, always learning from Him, as the disciples did.

Will we learn in Heaven? Definitely. We're told that in the coming ages God will continuously reveal to us the "incomparable riches of his grace" (Ephesians 2:7). When we die, we'll know a lot more than we do now, but we'll keep learning about God and His creation and each other throughout eternity!

What is the essence of eternal life? "That they may know you, the only true God, and Jesus Christ, whom you have sent" (John 17:3). The best part of Heaven will be knowing and enjoying God. All our explorations and adventures and projects in the eternal Heaven—and I believe there will be many—will pale in comparison to the wonder of being with God and entering into His happiness. Yet everything else we do will help us to know and worship God better.

We only look forward to what we can imagine. So picture yourself and loved ones who know Jesus, walking together on the New Earth. All of you have powerful bodies, stronger than those of Olympic decathletes. You are laughing, playing, talking., and reminiscing. You reach up and pluck an apple or an orange. You take a bite. It's so sweet that it's startling. You've never tasted anything so good. Now you see someone coming toward you. It's Jesus, with a big smile on His face. You fall to your knees in worship. He pulls you up and embraces you. Could anything be better than the place the Carpenter from Nazareth has been preparing for us for two thousand years?

As we continue to look in Scripture, we can learn more about what it will be like for God to dwell with us and about our relationship with Him.

8. Read Leviticus 26:9–13; Ezekiel 37:24–28; 2 Corinthians 6:14–18; and Revelation 21:1–4, 22–27; 22:12–14. What pictures do these Scriptures paint of what it will be like for God to live with us? What kind of access will we have to God?

9. Read Isaiah 25:6–8; Matthew 20:25–28; Luke 12:37; John 13:3–17. What do you think or feel about the idea of our Lord serving us in Heaven? Compare this to traditional images of Heaven many people have. What's different? What does that mean for how we should live our lives now?

When you picture Heaven, do you cringe at the thought of an eternal, boring church service? That notion doesn't come from God but from the devil. We will worship in Heaven, but there will be nothing boring about it. It will be a magnificent celebration!

In fact, all that we do will be an act of worship, whether we're riding a bike, reading a book, writing a song or taking a walk. Have you ever spent a day or several hours when you sensed the presence of God as you hiked, worked, gardened, drove, read, or did the dishes? Those are foretastes of Heaven—not because we are doing nothing but worshipping, but because we are worshipping God as we do everything else.

10. Read Genesis 47:31; Exodus 33:9–11; 1 Kings 1:46–48; Nehemiah 9:3; Daniel 7:13–14; 1 Thessalonians 5:16–18; Revelation 4–5; 7:9–12. What are some of the characteristics of the worship described in these passages? Who is worshipping and how are they doing it?

11. How is worship a part of our relationship with God now? From what we see in the Bible and in our own experience, what might we expect worship to be like, and what will its purpose be on the New Earth?

Reflection

You may wish to use a worship song ("Praise the King" is provided in the *Video Series*) to help people focus as they spend a few minutes reflecting on God in Heaven. Here are some Scriptures and thoughts to help you:

- Think about a desire or longing you have had, even today. Imagine how that longing might be fulfilled in the New Earth.
- Read Hebrews 12:22–23. What does it mean to you to know that, when you accepted Christ as your Savior, you became part of Heaven's community?
- Pray, asking God to help you understand your earthly desires and joys in the light of the primary joy we will have through the presence of God in the future Heaven.
- Commit to reading the Scriptures presented below.

Response

Use the ideas and questions presented here in your personal time with God this week:

- What is one thought from this session that has given you some peace or made something clearer to you about Heaven?

- Read these verses about the glory of God. Jot down any phrases, thoughts, or images that stand out to you.

    1 Chronicles 16:28–30

    Psalm 29:3

    Psalm 72:18–19

    Habakkuk 2:14

Luke 2:9

John 17:24

Numbers 14:20–24

Isaiah 40:5; 59:19

Ezekiel 1:28

1 Thessalonians 2:19

• Use David's prayer in Psalm 27:4–14 to guide your prayer
  time. Ask God to shape your desire to seek Him and want
  to be with Him. Remember that God is your safe place in
  times of trouble, and that you can look forward to living
  with Him when He dwells with us on the New Earth. Ask
  God to teach you to follow His straight path—to know
  His truth. Be thankful for His promises and be encour-
  aged as you wait for the Lord.

LIVING IN HEAVEN

Then all your people will be righteous and they will possess the land forever.

Isaiah 60:21

Preparation

Concepts in this session are covered in depth in Chapters 9, 10, 14–16 of *Heaven*. Specific questions on our bodies and activities in Heaven are addressed in Chapters 28–33. We'll also be studying the following Scriptures: Isaiah 60; Genesis 1:27–28; Matthew 25:34; Revelation 22:1–5; Genesis 3:14–24; Isaiah 65:17–19, 21, 25; 1 Corinthians 15:35–58; and Romans 8:9–11.

Leader tip: Communicate with your group to make sure they are aware of these resources. If you will be using the video teaching and/or the worship song provided on the *Heaven: The Official Study Guide Video Series*, check to see if the host of the group has appropriate video equipment.

Connection

As you begin this session, let a volunteer open with a brief prayer for your time together. If there are newcomers, introduce them to the group. If you have a large group, you may want to divide into smaller groups of two or three for the Connection activity.

Ask the groups to talk about their answers to these questions, then let some share the highlights of those discussions with the entire gathering:

- Describe your daily routine to someone (preferably someone who doesn't live with you).
- Help each other to categorize your daily activities into these areas: things you do intentionally for God, things you do for others, and things you do for yourself.
- In which category do most of your activities seem to fall? Are the objectives of your daily routine clear or unclear to you? Why?

Video Teaching

If you have the *Heaven: The Official Study Guide Video Series*, watch Session 4 now. Before pressing play, make sure everyone is in a position from which they can see and hear the video well. You may wish to use the provided worship song at the beginning of your time to focus attention or at the end to offer space for reflection—or both!

Discussion

We cannot anticipate or desire what we cannot imagine. That's why, I believe, God has given us glimpses of Heaven in the Bible—to fire up our imagination and kindle a desire for Heaven in our hearts.

Everything pleasurable we know about life on Earth we have experienced through our senses. So, when Heaven is portrayed as beyond the reach of our senses, it doesn't invite us; instead, it alienates and even frightens us. Our misguided attempts to make Heaven "sound spiritual" (i.e., non-physical) merely succeed in making Heaven sound unappealing. And that's why Satan will always discourage our imagination—or misdirect it to ethereal notions that violate Scripture. As long as the resurrected universe remains either undesirable or unimaginable, Satan succeeds in sabotaging our love for Heaven.

So look out a window. Take a walk. Imagine all of this world in its original condition. The happy dog with the wagging tail, not the snarling beast, beaten and starved. The flowers unwilted, the grass undying, the blue sky without pollution. People smiling and joyful, not angry, depressed, and empty. If you're not in a particularly beautiful place, close your eyes and envision the most beautiful place you've ever been—complete with palm trees, raging rivers, jagged mountains, waterfalls, or snow drifts.

In the last session we talked about what our relationship with God will be like when we are face to face with Him. In this session we'll learn more about what the prophets have to tell us about Heaven, about God's plan for an earthly kingdom, and how it relates to what John describes in Revelation. These passages help us create a picture of what our lives on the New Earth will look like.

1. Look at Isaiah 60. This passage does not contain the term *New Earth*, but we know it is related to that concept because John used some of the very same language to depict the New Earth in Revelation 21–22. Read Isaiah 60:1–6. Make a list of the nouns that are mentioned here, telling us who and what comprises the New Earth.

2. Note that nations and kings are mentioned here. What clue does that offer about life in the eternal Heaven?

3. Read Isaiah 60:11, 17–22. What do these images about the structure and materials of the place called "Zion" tell us about what life in the New Earth might be like? What parts of the life we experience now are missing from the life described in these verses? What parts are the same as or similar to what we experience now?

Isaiah's prophecies speak of an eternal kingdom, a messianic reign over a renewed Earth that lasts forever, on which sin, curse, and death have no place at all.

Why should we expect them to be literally fulfilled? Because his detailed prophecies regarding the Messiah's first coming were literally fulfilled (e.g., Isaiah 52:13; 53:4-12). When Jesus spoke to His disciples before ascending to Heaven, He said it was not for them to know *when* He would restore God's

Kingdom on Earth (Acts 1:6-8), but He did not say they wouldn't know *if* He would restore God's Kingdom. After all, restoring the Kingdom of God on Earth was His ultimate mission.

4.   Compare these passages: Genesis 1:27–28; Isaiah 60:21; Matthew 25:34; Revelation 22:1–5. Who is giving power in these passages, and to whom is it being given? What is the power for?

5.   These passages all describe life in a world that is free from what?

6. Under the curse, human culture has been severely hampered by sin, death, and decay. Read Genesis 3:14–24. Imagine the world as it is now depicted in one of those movie scenes in which everything is played in reverse. What would reversing the curse mean for our lives? What would that look like?

The evidence of the curse is all around us and even within us. But though the curse is real, it is *temporary*. Jesus will reverse the curse. Earth won't merely be put out of its misery; Christ will infuse it with a far greater life. Then, at last, it will become all God intended it to be.

If the present Earth under the curse can seem so beautiful and wonderful, if our bodies, so weakened by the curse, at times feel overcome with a sense of the Earth's majesty and splendor—then *how magnificent will the New Earth be?* And what will it feel like to enjoy it in perfect bodies? God promises that every one of His children will one day experience the answers to those questions.

7. Read Isaiah 65:17–19, 21, 25. What do these verses tell us about what we might be able to do and witness in the New Earth?

8. Read 1 Corinthians 15:35–58 and Romans 8:9–11. What are some of the differences between our current bodies and our resurrected bodies?

9. What are some common misconceptions or images people sometimes speak of about living in Heaven that are *not* backed up by Scripture?

Reflection

You may wish to use a worship song ("Revelation Song" is provided in the *Video Series*) to help people focus as they spend a few minutes reflecting on Heaven. Here are some Scriptures and thoughts to help you:

• Think about your daily routine that you described at the start of this session. What do you imagine your daily routine will look like in the ultimate Heaven centered on the New Earth? What will you look forward to? What will be the purpose of those activities?

- Read 2 Corinthians 5:4–5. Think about the kind of "groaning" and burdens you or others you have known have experienced. What about those experiences has pointed you toward thinking about the life to come? What do you think it means that we have the Spirit as a "deposit"?
- Pray, asking God to open your eyes to the truth about Heaven that we can find in His Word. Ask God to help you to let go of any language or imagery about Heaven or Hell that is unbiblical or not beneficial.
- Commit to reading the Scriptures below.

Response

Use the ideas and questions presented here in your personal time with God this week:

- What is one thought from this session that has given you some peace or made something clearer to you about Heaven?

- Read Hebrews 11:13–16, 39–40. Review the prophecies in Isaiah regarding the new heavens and earth in Isaiah 60, 62, 65, and 66. What better country are you longing for?

Write or draw about the imagery or promises that help you envision your eternal home.

- Read Revelation 4:11 and use it to shape your prayer time. Think of why our God is worthy. What has He done for you that makes Him worthy of the honor you give Him? Thank God for what He has done. Ask for forgiveness for the times you have not given Him honor, and ask Him to help you glorify Him in all you do each day.

PEACE FOR TODAY

Brothers and sisters, we do not want you to be uninformed about those who sleep in death, so that you do not grieve like the rest of mankind, who have no hope.

1 Thessalonians 4:13

Preparation

Concepts about human bodies, identities, relationships, and other aspects of our existence in Heaven are covered in depth in Chapters 28–38 of *Heaven*. We will touch on just a few of these aspects in this session. We'll also be studying the following Scriptures: 2 Corinthians 3:17–18; Philippians 3:20–21; Job 19:26–27; Luke 24:13–48; John 20:11–29; 21:1–14; Acts 1:1–3, 9–11; 2:29–36; 1:12–26; 1 Thessalonians 2:17–20; 3:6–10; 4:13–18; Zechariah 9:9–10; Ezekiel 37:26–28; Isaiah 42:1–4; Matthew 12:18–21.

Leader tip: Communicate with your group to make sure they are aware of these resources. If you will be using the video teaching and/or the worship song provided on the *Heaven: The Official Study Guide Video Series*, check to see if the host of the group has appropriate video equipment.

Connection

As you begin this session, let a volunteer open with a brief prayer for your time together. If there are newcomers, introduce them to the group. If you have a large group, you may want to divide into smaller groups of two or three for the Connection activity.

Ask the groups to talk about their answers to these questions, then let some share the highlights of those discussions with the entire gathering:

- Imagine you are a child again and you are put into a situation in which you must walk into a room full of children you don't know. What are your thoughts and feelings? If you ever had an experience like this, talk about what it was like. If you experienced anxiety, what was the reason for that anxiety?
- What would it take for you to feel peace in such a situation?

Video Teaching

If you have the *Heaven: The Official Study Guide Video Series*, watch Session 5 now. Before pressing play, make sure everyone is in a position from which they can see and hear the video well. You may wish to use the provided worship song at the beginning of your time to focus attention or at the end to offer space for reflection—or both!

Discussion

Over the years, two of the most common questions I've received about Heaven are 1) Will I still be me in Heaven? and 2) Will I recognize and know others?

Studying what Scripture says about Heaven can relieve our fears and allow us to experience the peace that Jesus promises His followers: "Peace I leave with you; my peace I give you. I do not give to you as the world gives. Do not let your hearts be troubled and do not be afraid" (John 14:27). May we remember that Jesus came to deliver us from the fear of death, "so that by his death he might destroy him who holds the power of death—that is, the devil—and free those who all their lives were held in slavery by their fear of death" (Hebrews 2:14-15).

The Carpenter from Nazareth is preparing a place for us. He knows how to build. He's constructed entire worlds, billions of them. He's going to strip the damaged paint off the old Earth, remove the dents and scars refinish it, and present it magnificent and pristine. He says it will one day be our home . . . and *His*, for He will dwell there with His people, bringing Heaven to Earth (Revelation 21:3).

1. Read 2 Corinthians 3:17–18 and Philippians 3:20–21. What kinds of transformations are described in these verses?

2. Read Job 19:26–27 and Luke 24:39. Write down or circle the phrases in these two passages that emphasize individual recognition.

3. Have you ever heard people from other religions, or even other Christians, talking about what our lives will be like in Heaven? What are some other concepts you've heard about our existence after death? How do those representations compare to what we've seen in the Bible through this study?

Though we become new people when we come to Christ, with new hearts, we still remain the same people. Similarly, when our bodies are resurrected, and we enter the New Earth, we will be the same people.

Job said, "After my skin has been destroyed, yet in my flesh I will see God; I myself will see him with my own eyes—I, and not another" (Job 19:26-27). Just as Job will be Job in the resurrection, so you will be you, and I will be me—but without any of the bad parts!

Think about it. The resurrected Jesus did not become someone else; He remained who He was before His resurrection. When John was fishing with some of the other disciples, he saw Jesus on the seashore and said, "It is the Lord!" (John 21:7). So you will still recognize friends and family, and they will recognize you, too.

4. Read Luke 24:13–48; John 20:11–29; and 21:1–14. What do these post-resurrection appearances of Jesus imply about our ability to know one another on the New Earth? What do they tell us about what will continue to be the same about our resurrected selves?

5. Read Acts 1:1–3, 9–11; 2:29–36. What were the disciples told about where Jesus had gone? What did they tell others?

6. Read Acts 1:12–26. After Jesus was gone, we see His followers gathering together once again in the upper room. What kinds of things did they do? What were they not doing?

Who of us hasn't been touched by death? A dear friend of mine died at age 19 in a terrible farm accident. My uncle was murdered. My mother was suddenly taken by cancer. Eleven years later, to the day, I was holding the hand of my closest friend when he died at age 38. My wife and daughters and brother and I were with my father when he died. My wife's dear mother and father have died. Karen Stout Coleman, a beloved coworker at EPM, our ministry, died just a month ago as I write. On and on it goes. Your list is likely as long as mine, maybe longer.

But here is the good news, and it is breathtaking: one day God "will swallow up death forever" (Isaiah 25:7). All that is wrong will be made right. "No longer will there be any curse" (Revelation 22:3).

When death comes to take away someone we love, we grieve—and rightly so. But for the believer, that grief is infused with hope. Our loved ones are not truly lost—after all, we know where they are, and we will see them again.

Jesus said, "Blessed are you who weep now, for you will laugh. . . . Rejoice in that day and leap for joy, because great is your reward in heaven" (Luke 6:21-23). This is the promise of God: His children who weep now at all their losses, will laugh in Heaven.

For those who know Christ, death is, at worst, a temporary separation. Our relationships cannot be terminated, only interrupted. What will eventually follow—whether in hours, days, years, or decades—is a great reunion, wonderful beyond imagination.

7. Read 1 Thessalonians 2:17–20; 3:6–10; 4:13–18. What do these verses tell us about the character of the relationships that Paul is talking about? What brought them joy? What was reassuring to them?

8. Read the following verses that talk about the establishing of peace on Earth: Zechariah 9:9–10; Ezekiel 37:26–28; Isaiah 42:1–4; Matthew 12:18–21. What made this peace possible? Who was the architect of peace? What do promises of peace on Earth tell us about the life to come?

Reflection

You may wish to use a worship song ("Before the Throne of God" is provided in the *Video Series*) to help people focus as they spend a few minutes reflecting on Heaven. Here are some Scriptures and thoughts to help you focus:

- Imagine a place where you feel very much at home or at peace. You've just had a very busy, very stressful day, and you walk in the door. What feelings do you have? What about this place makes you feel at home? Have you ever thought of Heaven as your home?
- Read Matthew 26:36–38; John 11:33–35, 12:26–28. What do these verses tell you about Jesus? What does it mean to know that Jesus—though He was from Heaven and was sure of Heaven—still felt sorrow and grief?
- Pray, asking God to help you find peace and comfort in your knowledge of Heaven.
- Commit to reading the Scriptures presented below.

Response

Use the ideas and questions presented here in your personal time with God this week:

- What is one thought from this session that has given you some peace or made something clearer to you about Heaven?

- Study what these verses have to say about suffering. Write about what you learn from them:

  Romans 8:18

  Luke 6:22–23

  Colossians 1:24

  James 1:2–4

  Luke 10:19–20

  1 Peter 4:12–19

- Make Philippians 4:6–8 into a prayer. Ask God to help you not be anxious about anything—think about or write out a list of anything that is currently causing anxiety in you. Under each of those items, write out a bullet-point request and a bullet-point thank-you to God. For example, you could list "a broken relationship" and under that list these points: 1) Please help me forgive my friend. 2) Thank you for showing me forgiveness.

HOPE FOR TOMORROW

*For everything that was written in the past was written to teach
us, so that through the endurance taught in the Scriptures and
the encouragement they provide we might have hope.*

Romans 15:4

Preparation

Concepts in this session are spread throughout the *Heaven* book but covered in depth in Chapters 21–23 and 43–46 of *Heaven*. We'll also be studying the following Scriptures: 1 John 1; 3:1–4; Matthew 25:14–21, 24–30; Revelation 2:10, 26; 3:11, 21; Philippians 3:13–14, 7–11; Hebrews 11:16.

Leader tip: Communicate with your group to make sure they are aware of these resources. If you will be using the video teaching and/or the worship song provided on the *Heaven: The Official Study Guide Video Series*, check to see if the host of the group has appropriate video equipment.

Connection

As you begin this session, remind everyone that this is your last session for this study. Let a volunteer open with a brief prayer for your time together. If you have a large group, you may want to divide into smaller groups of two or three for the Connection activity.

Ask the groups to talk about their answers to these questions, then let some share the highlights of those discussions with the entire gathering:

- What was the last event—a visit with a friend, a show, a vacation, etc.—that you really looked forward to?
- Why did you look forward to it? What about it appealed to you the most?
- Imagine if you could capture all the best parts of that event—the good feelings, the pleasant people, the surprising joys, etc.—and relive them over and over again, whenever you wished.
- Better yet, suppose you had waiting for you new events and new adventures with Jesus and His people in His new creation, far better than anything you've ever known. Suppose you knew that the best was yet to be, that you will never pass your peak because you won't reach your peak until the resurrection, and after that there will be no more sin, suffering, deterioration or death. What you are supposing is exactly what God promises us in His Word! Right when we may start to think "It doesn't get any better than this" . . . it will!

Video Teaching

If you have the *Heaven: The Official Study Guide Video Series*, watch Session 6 now. Before pressing play, make sure everyone is in a position from which they can see and hear the video well. You may wish to use the provided worship song at the beginning of your time to focus attention or at the end to offer space for reflection—or both!

Discussion

Once we understand that all we love about the old Earth will be ours on the New Earth—either in the same form or another—we won't regret leaving all the wonders of the world we've seen or not yet seen. Why? Because we will yet be able to see them.

When we think of Heaven as unearthly, our present lives seem unspiritual, like they don't matter. When we grasp the reality of the New Earth, our present, earthly lives suddenly matter. Conversations with loved ones matter. The taste of food matters. Work, leisure, creativity, and intellectual stimulation matter. Rivers and trees and flowers matter. Laughter matters. Service matters. Why? Because they are eternal. Life on Earth matters not because it's the only life we have, but precisely because it isn't—it's the beginning of a life that will continue without end. Understanding Heaven doesn't just tell us what to do, but why. What God tells about our future lives enables us to interpret our past and serve Him in our present.

1. Is resurrected living in a resurrected world with the resurrected Christ and His resurrected people your daily longing and hope? If not, what could help you to focus on this daily? What is distracting you from this focus?

2. Read 1 John 1. What does this chapter tell us about walking in darkness? What was your life like before you knew Jesus?

3. Read 1 John 3:1–4. How can focusing on what will happen when Christ comes help us?

Christ is not simply preparing a place for us; He is preparing us for that place. Right now, on this Earth, we are burdened by sin and by the consequences of past sins. But the hope we are living for is not just freedom from those consequences—it's complete deliverance from sin. When we are released from the bondage of the curse of sin, we will be free to become fully functioning humans—created in God's image. On the New Earth, we'll do whatever we want, because we'll want whatever God wants!

Heaven should affect our activities and ambitions, our recreation and friendships, and the way we spend our money and time. If I believe I'll spend eternity in a world of unending beauty and adventure, will I be content to spend all my evenings staring at game shows, sitcoms, and ball games? Even if I keep my eyes off of impurities, how much time will I want to invest in what doesn't matter? Spending time in God's Word and investing in people will pay off in eternity and bring me joy and perspective now.

Following Christ is not a call to abstain from gratification but to delay gratification. It's finding our joy in Christ rather than seeking joy in the things of this world. Heaven—our assurance of eternal gratification and fulfillment—should be our North Star, reminding us where we are and which direction to go.

When we realize the pleasures that await us in God's presence, we can forgo lesser pleasures now. When we realize the possessions that await us in Heaven, we will gladly give away possessions on Earth to store up treasures in Heaven (Matthew 6:19-21). When we realize the power offered to us as rulers in God's Kingdom, a power we could not handle now but will handle with humility and benevolence then, we can forgo the pursuit of power here.

To be Heaven-oriented is to be goal-oriented in the best sense.

4. Read Matthew 25:14–21. What does the master say to the servant? What would the servant share in?

5. Read vv. 24–30. What was the problem with the servant who received just the one bag? Where did he go wrong?

6. What does this parable tell you about what your focus should be as you live on this present Earth?

The idea of entering into the Master's happiness is a telling picture of Heaven. It's not simply that being with the Master produces joy in us, though certainly it will. Rather, it's that our Master himself is happy. He takes joy in Himself, in His children, and in His creation. His joy is contagious. Once we're liberated from the sin that blocks us from God's happiness and our own, we'll enter into His happiness. Joy will be the very air we breathe. The Lord is inexhaustible—therefore His joy is inexhaustible.

For some of us, hanging onto the hope of that joy can be difficult. If you are reading this book right now and feeling that the end of your own life may come very soon, you may be troubled, feeling uncertain or unready to leave. Make sure of your relationship with Jesus Christ. Be certain that you're trusting Him alone to save you—not anyone or anything else, and certainly not any good works you've done. And then allow yourself to get excited about what's on the other side of death's door. Remember that the world there is just as real as the world you are sitting in right now—you just can't see it yet.

If you are depressed and wondering if you can escape from this world, don't give up. Don't desert your post. If you are still here, God has a purpose for you. Don't listen to the whispers of Satan that may try to tell you something different. Satan is a liar and a murderer (John 8:44; 1 Peter 5:8). He wants to destroy. Seek the truth-teller. Listen to Jesus. Through our suffering, the difficulties we are enduring, and even our moments of depression, God is preparing us for a new world. He's expanding our capacity for eternal joy.

By God's grace, use the time you have left on the present Earth to store up for yourself treasures on the New Earth, to be laid at Christ's feet for His glory (Revelation 4:10). Then look forward to meeting in Heaven Jesus Himself, as well as those touched by your Christ-exalting choices.

7. Read Revelation 2:10, 26; 3:11, 21. What promises are stated in these verses?

8. Read Philippians 3:13–14 and then look back at vv. 7–11. What goal is Paul pressing on toward? Think about what you spend most of your time doing. What goal is your life moving toward?

9. Read Hebrews 11:16. How does God feel about those who focus on Heaven? Don't let a day go by without anticipating the new world that Christ is preparing for us. God loves the Heaven-bound, and He is proud of the Heaven-minded.

Reflection

You may wish to use a worship song ("As It Is in Heaven" is provided in the *Video Series*) to help people focus as they spend a few minutes reflecting on Heaven. Here are some Scriptures and thoughts to help you:

- Imagine you are at a party. It's the best party you've ever been to—the best food, the best friends, the best laughs. But just when things seem to be getting really good, you realize it is time to go and someone drags you away. You absolutely hate the idea of leaving. It's even depressing. But once you arrive home, you open the door and—surprise! An even better party is happening inside! The food is better, the music is happier, and all of your best friends in the world are there. And the best part is, the party never ends. What do you think about that? How do you feel? How is this never-ending party something like our lives in Heaven?

- Read Romans 8:14–25. Who are we heirs with? What is our inheritance? What are we waiting for? In what hope were we saved?
- What are three practical actions you can take to intentionally focus on Heaven and "things above" this week?
- Thank God for His incomparable glory and for giving us gifts that are better than anything we can imagine. Ask Him to help you continue to transform your vision of this world so that you see it through the lens of eternity.
- Commit to answering the questions presented below.

Response

Use the ideas and questions presented here in your personal time with God this week:

- What is one thought from this session that has given you some peace or made something clearer to you about Heaven?

At the end of *Heaven*, I offer some questions to help us daily train ourselves to be Heaven-minded. As you work to focus your mind on things above, ask yourself these questions:

- Do I daily reflect on my own mortality?

- Do I daily realize there are only two destinations—Heaven or Hell—and that I and every person I know will go to one or the other?

- Do I daily remind myself that this world is not my home and that everything in it will burn, leaving behind only what's eternal?

- Do I daily recognize that my choices and actions have a direct influence on the world to come?

- Do I daily realize that my life is being examined by God, the Audience of One, and that the only appraisal of my life that will ultimately matter is His?

- Do I daily reflect on the fact that my ultimate home will be the New Earth, where I will see God and serve Him as a resurrected being in a resurrected human society, where I will overflow with joy and delight in drawing nearer to God by studying Him and His creation, and where I will exercise, to God's glory, dominion over His creation?

- Read Psalm 37 and make it your prayer today.

SESSION 1 PRAYERS

REQUESTS	PRAISES

SESSION 1 PRAYERS

REQUESTS   PRAISES

SESSION 2 PRAYERS

REQUESTS | PRAISES

SESSION 2 PRAYERS

REQUESTS | PRAISES

SESSION 3 PRAYERS

REQUESTS | PRAISES

SESSION 3 PRAYERS

REQUESTS | PRAISES

SESSION 4 PRAYERS

REQUESTS	PRAISES

SESSION 4 PRAYERS

REQUESTS | PRAISES

SESSION 5 PRAYERS

REQUESTS | PRAISES

SESSION 5 PRAYERS

REQUESTS

PRAISES

SESSION 6 PRAYERS

REQUESTS	PRAISES

SESSION 6 PRAYERS

REQUESTS	PRAISES

RECOMMENDED READING

50 Days of Heaven, by Randy Alcorn

Eternal Perspectives, by Randy Alcorn

Everything You Always Wanted to Know About Heaven, by Randy Alcorn

Heaven: Your Real Home, by Joni Eareckson Tada

Picturing Heaven, by Randy Alcorn

Surprised by Hope, by N.T. Wright

The Bible and the Future, by Anthony A. Hoekema

The Last Things (Death, Judgment, Heaven, and Hell), by Paul Helm

The Message of Heaven & Hell (The Bible Speaks Today Series), by Bruce Milne

The World to Come, by Isaac Watts

INDUCTIVE BIBLE STUDY

The following list of verses are provided for you to perform an inductive Bible study on the topic of Heaven. You may wish to do this on your own or as part of your group study.

An inductive study means that you look at passages of the Bible, read them, and study them within their context. You might want to read a passage and then look at the passages around it. Find out who is speaking and to whom. Use a Bible dictionary to understand words and phrases that might not mean the same to you as they did at the time of the person writing.

As you gain understanding, write down questions you have and observations you make. Look for patterns in your observations as you continue with the other passages. If you are doing this study as part of a group, bring your questions for discussion within the group. If you are doing the study on your own, seek out Bible scholars who may be able to help you answer your questions. On average, you should expect to spend at least 5-10 minutes on reading each passage and writing down what you learn from that passage.

The purpose of doing this particular study is to find out the breadth of what Scripture has to say on a subject that many people think the Bible doesn't say much about. An asterisk (*) indicates primary passages for study; you may wish to start with these and then go back to others. Enjoy your reading and learning about Heaven!

1. Genesis 1:1-5

2. * Genesis 1:24-31

3. * Genesis 2:7-10

4. Genesis 2:15-17

5. * Genesis 3:1-24

6. * Genesis 5:21-24

7. Genesis 9:7-17

8. Numbers 27:13

9.   Deuteronomy 26:15

10. * 2 Kings 2:11

11. * 2 Kings 6:12-17

12. * Job 19:23-27

13. Psalm 11:4-6

14. * Psalm 16:5-11

15. * Psalm 23:6

16. Psalm 27:4

17. * Psalm 116:15

18. * Ecclesiastes 3:11

19. * Ecclesiastes 12:5-7, 13-14

20. * Isaiah 9:6-7

21. Isaiah 14:1214

22. * Isaiah 25:6-9

23. Isaiah 26:17-21

24. Isaiah 60:15-22

25. * Isaiah 65:14-25

26. Isaiah 66:12-24

27. Jeremiah 31:34

28. * Ezekiel 47:1-12

29. * Daniel 2:34-45

30. * Daniel 7:1-38

31. * Daniel 10:5-14, 20-21

32. * Daniel 12:1-4, 13

33. Malachi 3:16

34. Matthew 6:9

35. * Matthew 6:19-21

36. * Matthew 8:11-12

37. * Matthew 10:28

38. Matthew 11:20-24

39. * Matthew 12:36

40. Matthew 13:40-42

41. Matthew 16:27

42. * Matthew 17:1-4

43. Matthew 18:8

44. * Matthew 18:10

45. Matthew 19:21

46. * Matthew 19:27-30

47. * Matthew 20:20-23

48. Matthew 22:13

49. Matthew 24:51

50. * Matthew 25:20-23

51. Matthew 25:30-32

52. * Matthew 25:41-46

53. * Matthew 26:29

54. * Matthew 27:52-53

55. Matthew 28:2

56. Mark 6:41

57. * Mark 9:41

58. * Mark 9:43,44

59. * Mark 10:29-30

60. * Mark 12:18-27

61. Luke 6:20-26

62. Luke 6:35

63. * Luke 9:31-32

64. Luke 9:51

65. * Luke 10:20

66. * Luke 12:33

67. * Luke 12:47-48

68. Luke 13:28

69. * Luke 14:12-14

70. Luke 14:15

71. * Luke 15:7,10

72. * Luke 16:1-9

73. * Luke 16:19-31

74. * Luke 19:17-19

75. Luke 22:18

76. * Luke 22:29-30

77. * Luke 23:32-43

78. * Luke 24:13-35

79. * Luke 24:36-45

80. * John 5:28-29

81. * John 6:33,42

82. John 11:11

83. John 11:33-46

84. John 13:36

85. * John 14:23

86. * John 20:19

87. * John 21:1-15

88. Acts 1:11

89. * Acts 3:19-21

90. * Acts 7:60

91. * Acts 9:3-5

92. * Acts 17:31

93. Romans 2:6

94. Romans 2:16

95. * Romans 8:18-23

96. * Romans 8:34

97. Romans 8:37-39

98. Romans 14:10-12

99. 1 Corinthians 2:9-10

100. * 1 Corinthians 3:12-15

101. * 1 Corinthians 4:5

102. * 1 Corinthians 6:2-3

103. * 1 Corinthians 13:12

104. 1 Corinthians 15:12-28

105. * 1 Corinthians 15:29-49

106. * 1 Corinthians 15:50-58

107. 2 Corinthians 4:7-18

108. * 2 Corinthians 5:1-10

109. * 2 Corinthians 12:2-6

110. * Galatians 6:9

111. * Ephesians 2:6-7

112. Ephesians 4:8-10

113. Ephesians 6:8

114. * Ephesians 6:12

115. * Philippians 1:20-26

116. Philippians 2:9-11

117. Philippians 3:13-14

118. * Philippians 3:19-4:1

119. * Colossians 3:15

120. Colossians 3:22-25

121. * 1 Thessalonians 4:13-18

122. * 2 Thessalonians 1:9

123. 1 Timothy 6:17-19

124. 2 Timothy 2:12

125. 2 Timothy 4:1

126. * 2 Timothy 4:6-8

127. * Hebrews 2:14-15

128. Hebrews 4:13

129. * Hebrews 8:5

130. * Hebrews 9:11; 23-24

131. * Hebrews 9:27

132. Hebrews 10:34-36

133. * Hebrews 11:8-10

134. * Hebrews 11:13-16

135. Hebrews 12:22-23

136. Hebrews 13:14

137. James 1:12

138. * 1 Peter 1:4

139. 1 Peter 1:12

140. * 2 Peter 3:7-14

141. * 1 John 3:2

142. 2 John 8

143. Revelation 2:10

144. * Revelation 2:17

145. Revelation 2:26-28

146. Revelation 3:4

147. * Revelation 3:11

148. Revelation 3:21

149. Revelation 4:9-11

150. * Revelation 5:8-10

151. Revelation 5:13-14

152. Revelation 6:2-8

153.   * Revelation 6:9-11

154.   * Revelation 7:9-12

155.   * Revelation 7:15-16

156.   Revelation 8:1

157.   Revelation 11:15

158.   Revelation 11:18

159.   * Revelation 11:19

160.   Revelation 12:7

161. * Revelation 13:6

162. Revelation 13:7-8

163. Revelation 14:10-11

164. * Revelation 14:13

165. Revelation 15:5-8

166. * Revelation 19:1-16

167. Revelation 20:5-6

168. Revelation 20:10

169. * Revelation 20:11-13

170. * Revelation 21:1-8

171. Revelation 21:9-21

172. * Revelation 21:22-27

173. * Revelation 22:1-6

174. Revelation 22:11-16

175. * Revelation 22:17-21

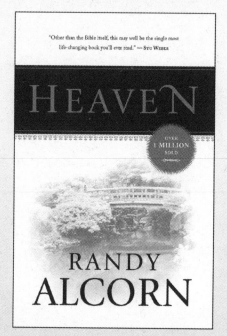